DELICIOUS GOUT

RECIPES WITH MEAT

PETER VOIT

Hi, I am Peter. I have been dealing on and off with Gout for well over a decade now. And I have learned over the years, that a healthy diet, and lifestyle is crucial for me as a Gout sufferer. I began eliminating all of the bad foods, and other foods that are not bad, but just trigger my Gout attacks. When I finally made a solid effort to do this. And it did take me a while to stick with it. I really noticed big changes in not just my Gout flairs. But also in my overall health. Which goes hand in hand. I want to share with you some of my best recipes that I create on a regular basis. I mix and match these recipes into my diet all throughout the year. And I live a pretty healthy lifestyle. Always consult with your Doctors to make sure that you can eat certain foods. Make sure the recipes do not have any foods that may not be best for you specifically. Enjoy!

Table of Contents

Lime Bean Salad

Stuffed Peppers

Stuffed Zucchini

Pickled Egg Salad

Herb Chicken and Mushrooms

Easy Chicken Salad

Potato Salad

Greek Salad

Walnut Chicken Salad

Chickpea and Eggplant Salad

Chicken Lasagna

Almond Broccoli Chicken Breast

Reducing Gout attacks
can begin in the kitchen.

Eliminating processed
foods. Refined sugars.
And making your own
meals from scratch.

Pinpointing and
eliminating foods that
trigger Gout attacks.

Each person is different.
With your Doctors help,
you can reduce Gout
attacks before they
begin.

Chicken Marinara

&

Bean Salad

INGREDIENTS

GREEN BEANS (1 ½ CUPS, CUT IN HALVES)

CANNED KIDNEY BEANS (1/4 CUP, DRAINED)

CIDER VINEGAR (2 TABLESPOONS)

PARSLEY (1 TEASPOON, DRIED)

BASIL (1 ½ TEASPOONS, DRIED)

TOMATO AND BASIL SAUCE (1/4 CUP)

VEGAN MOZZARELLA CHEESE (3 TABLESPOONS, SHREDDED)

CANNED GARBANZO BEANS (1/4 CUP, DRAINED)

COCONUT OIL (1 TEASPOON)

CHIVES (1 TEASPOON, DRIED)

BLACK PEPPER (1/2 TEASPOON)

CHICKEN BREAST (4 OZ.)

GARLIC POWDER (1/2 TEASPOON)

Directions

1. Set oven to 450°F.

2. Steam green beans until crisp preferably in a steamer. Combine green beans with kidney and chickpeas in a bowl.

3. In a small bowl add oil, chives, black pepper, vinegar, 1 teaspoon basil and parsley; whisk together and add to beans mixture. Toss to combine and chill for 30 minutes or until ready to serve.

4. Put chicken onto a piece of foil (large enough to wrap chicken). Add tomato sauce to chicken along with garlic powder, cheese and leftover basil.

5. Wrap chicken leaving a small opening. Place foil on a baking tray and bake for 20 – 40 minutes.

6. Serve chicken with bean salad.

Nutritional Info per Serving

Calories 368   Carbs 40g   Fat 12g   Protein 29g

Chicken Eggplant & Mushrooms

INGREDIENTS

CHICKEN THIGH   (4 OZ., GROUND)

EGGPLANT (1 CUP, PEEL REMOVED AND DICED)

BUTTON MUSHROOMS (1 CUP, SLICED)

RED CURRY PASTE (1 TABLESPOON)

EXTRA VIRGIN OLIVE OIL (2 TEASPOONS)

WHITE ONION (1/2 CUP, CHOPPED)

CANNED TOMATOES (1 ½ CUPS, DICED WITH LIQUID)

SEA SALT TO TASTE

BLACK PEPPER TO TASTE

DIRECTIONS

1. HEAT OIL IN A DEEP SKILLET AND COOK CHICKEN FOR 15 MINUTES UNTIL BROWNED ALL OVER.
2. ADD VEGETABLES AND CURRY PASTE, STIR TO COMBINE AND COVER WITH LID.
3. COOK OVER A LOW FLAME FOR 45 MINUTES, STIR OCCASIONALLY TO AVOID STICKING.
4. SERVE.

NUTRITIONAL INFO PER SERVING

CALORIES 339 CARBS 35G FAT 9G PROTEIN 32G

Easy Chinese Chicken Salad

INGREDIENTS:

2 CUPS OF ROMAINE LETTUCE – CHOPPED

½ CUP OF CILANTRO LEAVES – SHREDDED

¼ CUP OF SCALLIONS – CHOPPED

¼ CUP OF ALMONDS – UNSALTED, DRY TOASTED, SLICED

4 OUNCES OF CHICKEN BREAST – CANNED, CUBED

DIRECTIONS:

1. CHOP UP THE INGREDIENTS & TOSS ALL OF THE THEM TOGETHER.

2. ADD YOUR FAVORITE SPICES & APPLE CIDER VINEGAR FOR TOPPINGS.

NUTRITIONAL INFORMATION PER SERVING

CALORIES: 328 FAT: 15G CARBS: 9G PROTEIN: 32G

Spicy Chicken Stew – Slow Cooked

INGREDIENTS

CHICKEN BREASTS (20 OZ., WITHOUT SKIN AND BONES)

CANNED TOMATOES (40 OZ., DICED WITH JUICES)

CANNED BLACK BEANS (3/4 CUP, DRAINED)

GREEN BEANS (10 OZ.)

CILANTRO (1 TABLESPOON, CHOPPED)

CUMIN (1 TEASPOON)

COCONUT OIL (2 TABLESPOONS, EXTRA-VIRGIN)

RED ONION (1 ½ CUPS, CHOPPED)

GREEN SALSA (16 OZ.)

CANNED PINTO BEANS (15 OZ., DRAINED)

GREEN CHILI PEPPER (2 TEASPOONS)

DIRECTIONS

1. ADD ONIONS AND CHICKEN TO A SLOW COOKER AND TOP WITH TOMATOES, BLACK BEANS, GREEN BEANS, SALSA AND PINTO.

2. STIR TO COMBINE AND AD SEASONING, CHILI, CUMIN AND CILANTRO.

3. SET COOKER ON LOW AND COOK FOR 8–10 HOURS UNTIL MIXTURE IS SLIGHTLY THICKENED BUT NOT TOO THICK..

4. SERVE TOPPED WITH SEA SALT AND LEMON.

.NUTRITIONAL INFO PER SERVING

CALORIES 341   CARBS 37G   FAT 12G   PROTEIN 27G

Easy Side Salad

INGREDIENTS:

2 CUCUMBERS

4 TOMATOES

1 GREEN BELL PEPPER

1 TBSP. OF VIRGIN OLIVE OIL

3 TBSP. OF LEMON JUICE

DIRECTIONS:

1. DICE ALL OF THE VEGETABLES.

2. COMBINE ALL OF THE INGREDIENTS.

3. ADD SALT IF DESIRED AND SERVE WITH MEAL

This is an easy recipe that helps to get in some delicious veggies into you're diet. Which vegetables are great for overall health!

Studies have shown tart cherry juice to help reduce uric acid levels in the body! Making cherries a great choice for Gout!

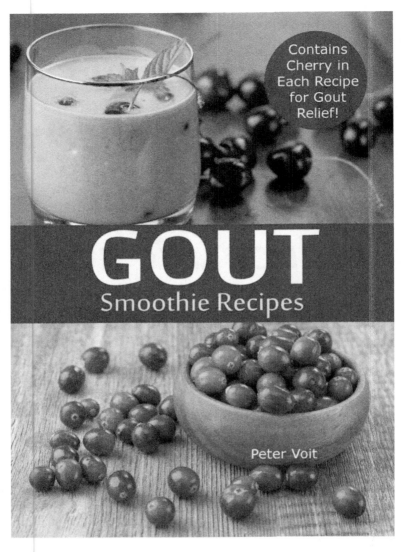

Contains Cherry in Each Recipe for Gout Relief!

GOUT
Smoothie Recipes

Peter Voit

CHECK OUT SOME OF MY BEST SMOOTHIE RECIPES

Anti - Inflammatory Spice Turmeric In Every Smoothie!

GOUT
Smoothie Recipes

Peter Voit

Delicious, & Healthy Plant Based Smoothies!

Chicken Mandarin With Spinach

INGREDIENTS

CHICKEN BREAST (4 OZ., COOKED, CUT INTO CUBES)

RED ONION (3/4 CUP, DICED)

FRENCH DRESSING (3 TABLESPOONS)

MANDARIN ORANGE (1/3 CUP)

MINT (1 TABLESPOON, FRESH, CHOPPED)

BABY SPINACH (1 CUP)

CELERY (1 CUP, DICED)

OLIVE OIL (2 TEASPOONS)

PEACH (1, PIT REMOVED AND SLICED)

TURMERIC (1/8 TEASPOON)

ROMAINE LETTUCE (1 CUP, CHOPPED)

DIRECTIONS

1. COOK CUBED CHICKEN BREAST ON A PAN WITH OIL FOR 15 – 30 MINUTES. UNTIL BROWNED. LET COOL 10 MINUTES.
2. ADD CELERY, OIL, PEACH, TURMERIC, MINT, CHICKEN, ONION, DRESSING AND ORANGES TO A BOWL; TOSS TO COMBINE.
3. ARRANGE SPINACH AND LETTUCE ON A DISH.
4. SERVE. MAY BE CHILLED.

NUTRITIONAL INFO PER SERVING

CALORIES 348 CARBS 22G FAT 11G PROTEIN 31G

Beef & Veggy Soup

INGREDIENTS

GROUND BEEF (12 OZ., 85% LEAN)

CARROTS (1 CUP, SLICED)

CANNED GARBANZO BEANS (1 CUP)

TOMATO PUREE (1/2 CUP)

BEEF BROTH (4 CUPS, NO SALT)

CHIVES (1/4 TEASPOON)

OREGANO (1/2 TEASPOON)

CELERY (2 ½ CUPS, DICED)

YELLOW ONION (1 CUP, CHOPPED)

TOMATOES (2 CUPS, CHOPPED)

OLIVE OIL (1 ½ TABLESPOONS)

GARLIC (4 CLOVES, CRUSHED)

PARSLEY (1 TEASPOON)

DIRECTIONS

1. HEAT OIL IN A LARGE POT AND ADD GARLIC, ONION AND TOMATOES; SAUTE FOR 5 MINUTES THEN ADD BEEF AND COOK FOR 5 MINUTES ON MED/HIGH. ADD ALL REMAINING INGREDIENTS AND STIR.

2. BRING MIXTURE TO A BOIL, THEN LOWER TEMP. COVER POT WITH LID TILTED AND COOK FOR 40 MINUTES TILL VEGETABLES ARE COOKED.

NUTRITIONAL INFO PER SERVING

CALORIES 257   CARBS 9G   FAT 11G   PROTEIN 29G

Garlic Beef & Red Lentils

INGREDIENTS

RED ONION (1/2 CUP, CHOPPED)

BAY LEAVES (2)

GROUND BEEF (7 OZ., 85% LEAN)

RED LENTILS (1 CUP, COOKED)

ITALIAN SEASONING MIX (OR MRS DASH)

OLIVE OIL (1 ½ TEASPOONS, EXTRA VIRGIN)

CELERY (1/2 CUP, CHOPPED)

GARLIC (2 – 4 CLOVES, CRUSHED)

CANNED TOMATOES (14.5 OZ., DICED)

BLACK PEPPER GROUND

DIRECTIONS

1. COOK LENTILS ACCORDING TO PACKAGE DIRECTIONS. TAKES 20 – 30 MINUTES.
2. HEAT OIL IN A SKILLET AND ADD BAY LEAVES, CELERY AND ONION FOR 3 MINUTES UNTIL SOFT AND TRANSLUCENT.
3. ADD GARLIC AND BEEF AND COOK FOR 15 MINUTES UNTIL BEEF IS GOLDEN ALL OVER. PUT IN TOMATOES AND COOKED LENTILS AND COOK FOR 5 MINUTES UNTIL THOROUGHLY HEATED.
4. ADD BLACK PEPPER AND ITALIAN SEASONING; STIR TO COMBINE.
5. SERVE.

NUTRITIONAL INFO PER SERVING

CALORIES 325 CARBS 33G FAT 11G PROTEIN 26G

Top Sirloin and Vegetable Stir Fry

INGREDIENTS

BASIL (1 TABLESPOON, CHOPPED)

PARSLEY (1 TABLESPOON, CHOPPED)

LEAN TOP SIRLOIN (3 OZ., CUBED)

BELL PEPPER (1/2, GREEN)

YELLOW SQUASH (1/2 CUP, CUBED)

TOMATO (3/4, CHOPPED)

OLIVE OIL (1/2 TEASPOON)

BALSAMIC VINEGAR (1 ½ TABLESPOONS)

GARLIC (2 TEASPOONS, DICED)

MINT (1 TABLESPOON, CHOPPED)

BLACK PEPPER

RED BELL PEPPER (1/2, RED)

ZUCCHINI (2 CUPS, CUBED)

SHIITAKE MUSHROOMS (1 CUP, SLICED)

DIRECTIONS

1. ADD VINEGAR, GARLIC, MINT, BLACK PEPPER, 1 TEASPOON OIL, BASIL AND PARSLEY TO A BOWL AND MIX TOGETHER.

2. PUT MEAT INTO MIXTURE AND COAT; COVER AND PLACE IN REFRIGERATOR FOR 4 HOURS OR OVERNIGHT IF PREFERRED.

3. SLICE UP ZUCCHINI, MUSHROOMS, TOMATOES, PEPPER AND SQUASH. HEAT A SKILLET AND COAT WITH COOKING SPRAY OR COCONUT OIL; ADD BEEF AND COOK BEEF FOR 10 – 15 MINUTES, THEN ADD VEGETABLES AND COOK FOR AN ADDITIONAL 5 MINUTES OR UNTIL VEGGIES ARE TENDER. MIX WELL AS COOKING.

4. SERVE.

NUTRITIONAL INFO PER SERVING

CALORIES 347   CARBS 16G   FAT 10G   PROTEIN 27G

Spicy Egg Salad

INGREDIENTS:

2 - 4 EGGS - HARD BOILED WITH YOLKS

2 MEDIUM SCALLIONS - CHOPPED FINE

1 TSP. OF GREEN CHILI PEPPERS - DRAINED, CHOPPED

1 TBSP. OF CILANTRO - MINCED

½ SMALL RED PEPPER - CHOPPED FINE

¼ TSP. OF SALT

1/8 TSP. OF PEPPER

DIRECTIONS:

1. PEEL THE EGGS AND MASH THEM WITH A FORK.

2. ADD IN THE REST OF THE INGREDIENTS AND MIX.

3. SERVE IT IN THE BELL PEPPER. OR ON TOAST.

NUTRITIONAL INFO PER SERVING

CALORIES: 224 FAT: 17G CARB 6G PROTEIN 15G

Eggs are a low in purines food. Making them a great choice for Gout.

Cashew Orange Chicken

INGREDIENTS

ORANGE JUICE (1/3 CUP)

OLIVE OIL (1 ½ TEASPOONS)

CHICKEN BREAST (6 OZ., BONELESS, CUBED)

CASHEW NUTS (2 TEASPOONS)

SOY SAUCE (2 TABLESPOONS)

GINGER (1/2 TEASPOON)

MANDARIN ORANGE (1 CUP)

GREEN BEANS (2 CUPS)

DIRECTIONS

1. COMBINE SOY SAUCE, GINGER, ORANGE JUICE AND HALF OF OIL IN A BOWL; ADD CHICKEN TO MIXTURE AND COAT. MARINATE FOR 30 MINUTES AT ROOM TEMPERATURE.

2. HEAT LEFTOVER OIL IN A SKILLET AND COOK CHICKEN FOR 15 MINUTES UNTIL THOROUGHLY COOKED.

3. COMBINE & ADD TO CHICKEN, STIR TO COMBINE AND COOK UNTIL THICK THEN ADD CASHEWS AND MANDARIN AND COOK UNTIL THOROUGHLY HEATED.

4. SERVE WITH GREEN BEANS.

NUTRITIONAL INFO PER SERVING

CALORIES 326   CARBS 35G   FAT 11G   PROTEIN 24G

Herbed Chicken

INGREDIENTS

OLIVE OIL (2 TEASPOONS)

APPLE CIDER VINEGAR (1 TABLESPOON)

GARLIC (1 – 3 CLOVES, CHOPPED)

WHITE ONION (1/2 CUP, CHOPPED)

ORANGE JUICE (1/4 CUP, FRESHLY SQUEEZED)

MANDARIN (1/2 CUP)

BRUSSELS SPROUTS (1/2 CUP)

CHICKEN BREAST (3 OZ., DICED)

PARSLEY (1 TABLESPOON, CHOPPED)

BUTTON MUSHROOMS (3 CUPS, SLICED)

WATER (2 TABLESPOONS)

ORANGE EXTRACT (1/2 TEASPOON)

DIRECTIONS

1. HEAT HALF OF OIL IN SKILLET AND ADD GARLIC, PARSLEY, CHICKEN AND VINEGAR; COOK FOR 10 MINUTES.

2. WHILE CHICKEN COOKS, HEAT LEFTOVER OIL IN ANOTHER SKILLET AND SAUTÉ MUSHROOMS AND ONION FOR 5 MINUTES.

3. ADD MANDARIN, ORANGE JUICE AND WATER TO CHICKEN AND COOK FOR 3 MINUTES; PREPARE SPROUTS.

4. COOK THEM IN OVEN AT 400F TEMP ON BAKING SHEET UNCOVERED 15 – 20 MINUTES. UNTIL BROWNED.

5. SERVE CHICKEN WITH SPROUTS AND MUSHROOMS MIXTURE.

NUTRITIONAL INFO PER SERVING

CALORIES 261   CARBS 9G   FAT 13G   PROTEIN 29G

Egg white Stuffed Mushroom

INGREDIENTS

PORTOBELLO MUSHROOMS (1, STEM REMOVED AND DICED)

MUSHROOMS (1 CUP, CHOPPED)

CELERY (1/4 CUP, CHOPPED)

RED BELL PEPPERS (1/4 CUP, CHOPPED)

TOMATO (1, CHOPPED)

VEGAN MOZZARELLA (1/4 CUP, SHREDDED)

OLIVE OIL (1 TEASPOON, EXTRA-VIRGIN)

WHITE ONION (1/2 CUP, CHOPPED)

ZUCCHINI (1, CHOPPED)

GARLIC (1 CLOVE, CRUSHED)

LENTILS (1/4 CUP, COOKED AND CRUSHED)

EGG WHITES LIQUID (1/2 CUP)

DIRECTIONS

1. SET OVEN TO 400°F.

2. HEAT A LARGE SKILLET AND COAT WITH COOKING SPRAY. ADD ONION, ZUCCHINI, GARLIC, MUSHROOMS, CELERY AND PEPPERS AND COOK FOR 8 MINUTES UNTIL TENDER; ADD TOMATOES TO MIXTURE.

3. PLACE PORTOBELLO INTO A GREASED BAKING PAN. BAKE FOR 5 MINUTES UNTIL SLIGHTLY TENDER.

4. ADD COOKED LENTILS, 2 TABLESPOONS OF CHEESE AND EGG WHITES TO VEGETABLES; STIR TO COMBINE & COOK EGG WHITES TILL FLUFFY.

5. TAKE PORTOBELLO FROM OVEN AND FILL WITH VEGETABLE MIXTURE, RETURN STUFFED PORTOBELLO TO OVEN AND BAKE FOR 15 MINUTES. REMOVE PORTOBELLO FROM OVEN, ADD CHEESE AND BAKE FOR AN ADDITIONAL 5 MINUTES.

6. SERVE.

NUTRITIONAL INFO PER SERVING

CALORIES 356   CARBS 22G   FAT 10G   PROTEIN 30G

Pecan Apple Salad

INGREDIENTS:

1 AVOCADO – CHOPPED

8 OUNCES OF CELERY – CHOPPED

2 LARGE APPLES – HONEY CRISP, CHOPPED

5 SCALLIONS – CHOPPED

3 OUNCES OF PECANS – CHOPPED

8 OUNCES OF CHICKEN – CANNED

2 LARGE TOMATOES – CHOPPED

1/2 CUCUMBER – CHOPPED

2 CUPS OF LETTUCE

1 OUNCE OF LEMON JUICE

1 OUNCE OF LIME JUICE

DIRECTIONS:

1. CHOP THE INGREDIENTS MINUS THE LETTUCE, AND THEN MIX THEM TOGETHER IN A LARGE MIXING BOWL.

2. ADD IN THE JUICES.

3. PLACE THE MIX ON TOP OF THE GREENS.

4. TOP IT WITH APPLE CIDER VINEGAR.

NUTRITIONAL INFORMATION PER SERVING

CALORIES: 524 FAT 27G CARB: 16G PRO 30G

Easy Chicken Salad

INGREDIENTS:

½ CUP OF COTTAGE CHEESE – LOW FAT

1 TSP. OF CURRY POWDER

DASH OF SALT

DASH OF PEPPER

2 SPRING ONIONS – LARGE

¼ CUP OF WALNUT HALVES – CHOPPED

1 SMALL GREEN APPLE – PEELED, CUBED

1 CUP OF CANNED CHICKEN BREAST – CHOPPED

DIRECTIONS:

1. PUREE THE COTTAGE CHEESE IN A BLENDER OR A FOOD PROCESSOR.

2. CHOP AND MIX THE APPLE, WALNUTS, ONION.

3. ADD IN THE CURRY POWDER, PEPPER, AND THE SALT. MIX IT VERY WELL.

4. SERVE ON A BED OF LETTUCE OR ON A PITA.

5. USE COTTAGE CHEESE AS DRESSING, OR MIX IN WITH OTHER INGREDIENTS.

NUTRITIONAL INFORMATION PER SERVING

CAL 197 FAT: 7G   CARB 6G   PROT 6G

Chicken Parmesan and Squash

INGREDIENTS

CHICKEN BREASTS (12 OZ., SKINLESS AND BONELESS)

GARLIC POWDER

TOMATO AND BASIL SAUCE (2 ½ CUPS)

ROSEMARY (DRIED)

BASIL (DRIED)

BLACK PEPPER

OLIVE OIL (1 TABLESPOON)

VEGAN MOZZARELLA (1/2 CUP, SHREDDED)

OREGANO (DRIED)

SPAGHETTI SQUASH (8 CUPS, COOKED)

DIRECTIONS

1. HEAT OVEN TO 400°F. SLICE SQUASH IN HALF LENGTHWISE AND SCOOP OUT SEEDS. SEASON WITH SALT. PLACE SQUASH CUT SIDE DOWN ON BAKING SHEET AND ROAST 45 MINUTES. USE A FORK TO SCRAPE OUT "SPAGHETTI."

2. SET OVEN TO 375F. USE GARLIC POWDER AND BLACK PEPPER TO SEASON CHICKEN.

3. HEAT OIL IN A SKILLET AND COOK CHICKEN FOR 20 MINUTES OR UNTIL THOROUGHLY COOKED.

4. PLACE CHICKEN INTO A BAKING DISH AND ADD HERBS, SAUCE AND CHEESE. BAKE FOR 10 MINUTES UNTIL CHEESE IS GOLDEN.

5. TAKE CHICKEN FROM SAUCE AND PLACE SAUCE INTO A DISH ALONG WITH SQUASH.

6. SERVE SQUASH WITH CHICKEN.

NUTRITIONAL INFO PER SERVING

CALORIES 359 CARBS 38G FAT 10G PROTEIN 30G

Rosemary Chicken

INGREDIENTS

GARLIC (1 CLOVE, CRUSHED)

VEGETABLE BROTH (1 CUP)

ROSEMARY (3 TEASPOONS, FRESH)

CHICKEN BREAST (6 OZ., BONELESS AND POUNDED)

CAULIFLOWER (4 CUPS)

OLIVE OIL (1 TEASPOON)

BABY SPINACH (10 CUPS)

ORGANIC BUTTER (1 TEASPOON)

VEGAN MOZZARELLA (1/4 CUP)

DIRECTIONS

1. HEAT OIL IN A SKILLET AND SAUTÉ GARLIC FOR 3 MINUTES UNTIL FRAGRANT.
2. ADD SPINACH, A TEASPOON OF ROSEMARY AND A ¼ OF BROTH; COVER POT AND COOK FOR 4 MINUTES UNTIL SPINACH IS WILTED.
3. IN ANOTHER SKILLET, MELT BUTTER AND COOK CHICKEN FOR 10 MINUTES OR UNTIL THOROUGHLY COOKED. TRANSFER CHICKEN TO POT WITH SPINACH.
4. COMBINE REMAINING BROTH AND ADD TO CHICKEN AND SPINACH. COOK UNTIL MIXTURE IS THICK. PREPARE CAULIFLOWER BY STEAMING.
5. TOP CHICKEN WITH CHEESE AND SERVE WITH CAULIFLOWER.

NUTRITIONAL INFO PER SERVING

CALORIES 389   CARBS 38G   FAT 13G   PROTEIN 31G

Salmon and Fruit Salsa

Ingredients

Wild caught Salmon (4 oz.)

Ginger (1 teaspoon, chopped)

Hot sauce

Blackberries (3/4 cup)

Green beans (1 ½ cups)

Soy sauce (2 teaspoons)

Dill (1/2 teaspoon)

Salsa (1/2 cup)

Blueberries (3/4 cup, slightly crushed)

Olive oil (1/2 teaspoon)

DIRECTIONS

1. COAT BAKING DISH WITH COOKING SPRAY OR OIL AND PUT SALMON INTO A PAN AND COOK ON MEDIUM UNTIL FINISHED.

2. COMBINE SOY SAUCE, DILL, HOT SAUCE AND GINGER IN A BOWL AND POUR OVER SALMON. STEAM GREEN BEANS SEPERATELY.

3. ADD FRUIT AND SALSA TO A BOWL AND GENTLY MIX TOGETHER, MASHING A LITTLE BIT.

4. SERVE FISH WITH SALSA AND GREEN BEANS.

NUTRITIONAL INFO PER SERVING

CALORIES 343 CARBS 37G FAT 10G PROTEIN 30G

Salsa Chicken

INGREDIENTS

CHICKEN BREAST (3 OZ.)

VEGAN MOZZARELLA (1 ½ TABLESPOONS)

GREEN BEANS (2 CUPS, STEAMED)

SALSA (1/2 CUP)

PEACH (1)

1 AVOCADO OR GUACAMOLE MIX

DIRECTIONS

1. SET OVEN TO 350F.

2. COAT BAKING DISH AND PLACE CHICKEN INTO DISH AND TOP WITH SALSA AND CHEESE.

3. BAKE FOR 20 MINUTES.

4. SERVE WITH BEANS, PEACH AND GUACAMOLE.

NUTRITIONAL INFO PER SERVING

CALORIES 343   CARBS 41G   FAT 10G   PROTEIN 29G

Research suggests to avoid such seafoods as shellfish, anchovies, sardines, scallops, herring, tuna, haddock, and more. However, Salmon has been labeled as a lower purine seafood. And a choice of many people with Gout. Make sure which seafoods you can eat, if any.

Cherry Tomato Salmon

INGREDIENTS

EGGPLANT (1, SLICED INTO ROUNDS)

OLIVE OIL (1 TEASPOON)

WILD CAUGHT SALMON (3.5 OZ.)

CHERRY TOMATOES (15, CUT INTO HALVES)

CURRY (1 TEASPOON)

BLACK PEPPER

SEA SALT

DILL

OLD BAY SEASONING (1 TEASPOON)

DIRECTIONS

1. SET OVEN AT 450F.

2. REMOVE STEM OF EGGPLANT AND SLICE INTO ROUND PIECES. USE FOIL TO LINE 2 BAKING TRAYS AND COAT WITH COOKING SPRAY.

3. COAT EGGPLANT WITH COOKING SPRAY THEN TOSS WITH BLACK PEPPER, SALT, AND CURRY; PLACE ONTO ONE OF THE LINED TRAYS. USE OIL TO COAT FISH AND SEASON WITH OLD BAY SEASONING.

4. PUT BOTH TRAYS INTO OVEN. BAKE EGGPLANTS FOR 3 – 5 MINUTES AND REMOVE FROM HEAT. ADD TOMATOES TO TRAY AND FLIP EGGPLANT PIECES AND COAT WITH COOKING SPRAY AGAIN. RETURN TRAY TO OVEN AND COOK FOR AN ADDITIONAL 3 – 5 MINUTES. TAKE SALMON AND VEGETABLES FROM OVEN. MAKE SURE SALMON IS FULLY COOKED. SHOULD NOT BE FROZEN SALMON.

5. SERVE WITH DILL.

NUTRITIONAL INFO PER SERVING

CALORIES 368   CARBS 41G   FAT 8G   PROT 29G

Chicken Basil Salad

INGREDIENTS:

3 TBSP. OF MAYONNAISE – FAT FREE

2 TBSP. OF LEMON JUICE

2 TSP. OF DIJON MUSTARD

1 TBSP APPLE CIDER VINEGAR

¼ TSP. OF HOT SAUCE

1/8 TSP. OF WHITE PEPPER

1 CUP OF CANNED CHICKEN BREASTS – CHOPPED

½ CUP OF CELERY – CHOPPED

¼ GREEN ONIONS – CHOPPED

¼ CUP OF BASIL

6 CUPS OF ROMAINE – SHREDDED

DIRECTIONS:

1. COMBINE YOUR FIRST FIVE INGREDIENTS AND MIX IT WELL.

2. COMBINE THE CHICKEN, GREEN ONIONS, CELERY, AND THE BASIL IN A MEDIUM MIXING BOWL.

3. ADD IN THE MAYONNAISE MIX AND TOSS IT GENTLY.

4. PLACE ONE CUP OF ROMAINE ON EACH PLATE.

5. SPRINKLE IT WITH PINE NUTS.

NUTRITIONAL INFORMATION PER SERVING

CALORIES: 254 FAT: 12G CARB 6G PRO 30G

Lime Bean Salad

INGREDIENTS:

1 CAN OF CORN

1 CUP OF CANNED BLACK BEANS

1 CUP OF CANNED CHICKPEAS

JUICE FROM 3 LIMES

2 TBSP. OF VIRGIN OLIVE OIL

4 TBSP. OF CUMIN

DIRECTIONS:

1. STRAIN ALL OF THE CANNED GOODS, AND RINSE.

2. PUT IT IN A LARGE SERVING BOWL.

3. ADD IN THE OIL AND CUMIN.

4. MIX IT WELL. ADD SALT IF DESIRED

NUTRITIONAL INFORMATION PER SERVING

CALORIES: 178   FAT: 7G   CARB 28G   PROT 6G

"Moderate portions of fish can be part of a gout diet. High-purine vegetables. Studies have shown that vegetables high in purines, such as asparagus and spinach, don't increase the risk of gout or recurring gout attacks."
mayoclinic.org

Stuffed Peppers

INGREDIENTS

OLIVE OIL (1 ½ TEASPOONS)

GARLIC (4 CLOVES, DICED)

CANNED KIDNEY BEANS (1/4 CUP)

2 HARDBOILED EGG

CELERY SALT (1/8 TEASPOON)

CHILI POWDER (1/8 TEASPOON)

HOT SAUCE (1/8 TEASPOON)

RED BELL PEPPERS TO LIKING

RED ONION (1 CUP, DICED)

MUSHROOMS (1 CUP, DICED)

TOFU (4 OZ., FIRM) OPTIONAL

DRY MUSTARD (1/2 TEASPOON)

CINNAMON (1/8 TEASPOON)

TURMERIC (1/8 TEASPOON)

DIRECTIONS

1. SET OVEN TO 400F.

2. HEAT OIL IN A SKILLET AND ADD ONION, MUSHROOMS, RED PEPPER, ONION AND KIDNEY BEANS. COOK FOR 5–10 MINUTES UNTIL VEGGIES ARE TENDER; TAKE FROM HEAT AND COOL.

3. TRANSFER COOLED VEGGIES TO A BOWL WITH TOFU, HOT SAUCE, EGGS AND SPICES; MIX TOGETHER UNTIL THOROUGHLY COMBINED.

4. REMOVE STEMS FROM BELL PEPPERS AND TAKE OUT SEEDS INSIDE.

5. COAT BAKING DISH AND STUFF PEPPERS WITH MIXTURE AND PLACE INTO DISH. USE FOIL TO COVER DISH AND BAKE FOR 60 MINUTES.

6. SERVE WARM.

NUTRITIONAL INFO PER SERVING

CALORIES 387   CARBS 44G   FAT 13G   PROTEIN 28G

Stuffed Zucchini

INGREDIENTS

RED ONION (1 CUP, SLICED THIN)

CARAWAY SEEDS (2 TEASPOONS)

ITALIAN CHICKEN SAUSAGE (2 LINKS)

SUMMER SQUASH (2 CUPS, SLICED IN HALF)

VEGETABLE BROTH (1 CUP, UNSALTED)

HOT SAUCE (1 TEASPOON)

PARSLEY (1/4 CUP, CHOPPED)

ZUCCHINI (3 CUPS, SLICED IN HALVES)

TOMATOES (3 CUPS, DICED)

VEGAN MOZZARELLA (1/3 CUP, SHREDDED)

DIRECTIONS

1. SET OVEN TO 375F.

2. HEAT A SKILLET AND ADD 2 TABLESPOONS OF BROTH, HOT SAUCE, PARSLEY, SAUSAGE, ONION AND CARAWAY SEEDS. COOK FOR 5 MINUTES OR UNTIL SAUSAGE IS GOLDEN ALL OVER; REMOVE FROM HEAT AND PUT ASIDE UNTIL NEEDED.

3. PLACE ½ OF SQUASH AND ZUCCHINI INTO A BAKING DISH AND FILL WITH SAUSAGE MIXTURE; REPEAT WITH LEFTOVER SQUASH AND ZUCCHINI.

4. ADD LEFTOVER BROTH, COVER WITH FOIL AND BAKE FOR 20 MINUTES. REMOVE FOIL, TOP WITH CHEESE AND BAKE FOR AN ADDITIONAL 10 MINUTES.

5. SERVE.

NUTRITIONAL INFO PER SERVING

CALORIES 345   CARBS 39G   FAT 11G   PROTEIN 28G

Pickled Egg Salad

INGREDIENTS:

5 WHOLE EGGS – BOILED

1/3 CUP OF MAYONNAISE LIGHT

1 TSP. OF MUSTARD

1 TBSP. OF PICKLE RELISH

¼ CUP OF GREEN ONION – CHOPPED

DIRECTIONS:

1. MIX ALL OF THE INGREDIENTS GENTLY. SERVE ON SPROUTED TOAST.

NUTRITIONAL INFORMATION PER SERVING

CALORIES: 524   FAT: 27G CARB 6G PROT 20G

Herb Chicken and Mushrooms

INGREDIENTS:

5 CUPS OF SHIITAKE MUSHROOMS

1 MEDIUM RED ONION – CHOPPED

1 MEDIUM CARROT – CHOPPED

¼ CUP OF TOMATO PIECES – DRIED

¾ CUP OF CHICKEN BROTH – REDUCED SODIUM

1 TSP. OF DRIED THYME – CRUSHED

½ TSP. OF DRIED BASIL – CRUSHED

½ TSP. OF SALT

¼ TSP. OF PEPPER

12 SMALL CHICKEN THIGHS – SKINNED

3 CUPS OF WHOLE WHEAT FETTUCCINI NOODLES – COOKED

FRESH BASIL – SNIPPED

DIRECTIONS:

1. IN YOUR SLOW COOKER COMBINE THE ONION, MUSHROOMS, CARROT, AND TOMATO PIECES. ADD THE CHICKEN BROTH. SPRINKLE THE THYME, SALT, PEPPER, AND DRIED BASIL.
2. COVER IT AND COOK IT ON LOW FOR 7–8 HOURS OR ON HIGH FOR 3 ½ – 4 HOURS.
3. TRANSFER THE CHICKEN AND THE VEGETABLES TO A PLATTER. SPOON THE LIQUID ON THE TOP.
4. SERVE IT WITH THE COOKED PASTA AS AN OPTION. GARNISH IT WITH THE FRESH BASIL.

NUTRITIONAL INFORMATION PER SERVING
CALORIES: 406 FAT: 17G CARB 19G PRO 33G

THIS SHOULD LAST SEVERAL DAYS. IF YOU DO NOT HAVE A SLOW COOKER YOU ARE MISSING OUT ON ONE OF THE BEST WAYS TO GET IN HEALTHY CHOICE MEALS! GET YOURSELF A SLOW COOKER, AND THANK ME LATER.

Easy Chicken Salad

INGREDIENTS:

4 CUPS OF ROMAINE LETTUCE

1 TOMATO – SLICED

½ TBSP. OF AMERICAN CHEESE – SHREDDED

½ CUP OF CANNED CORN

4 OUNCE OF CHICKEN BREAST – CANNED

DIRECTIONS:

1. CHOP YOUR LETTUCE.

2. ADD IN THE TOMATOES AND THE CHEESE.

3. ADD IN THE CORN.

4. MIX IT ALL TOGETHER.

5. SEASON WITH APPLE CIDER VINEGAR AND SALT.

NUTRITION INFO PER SERVING

CALS 130 FATS 3G CARB 4G PRO 12G

*Processed foods.
Refined sugars.
High trans fat foods.
All have been linked to
poor health. A healthy
diet should consist of a
wide variety of fruits
and vegetables. High
fructose corn syrup is a
no-no for anyone with
Gout.*

Potato Salad

INGREDIENTS:

2 POUNDS OF RED POTATOES – CUT INTO CUBES

½ RED ONION – SLICED THIN

½ CUP OF CHERRY TOMATOES – HALVED

¼ CUP OF BACON BITS – OPTIONAL

4 TBSP. OF BASIL

¼ CUP OF ITALIAN DRESSING

¼ CUP OF MAYONNAISE

2 TSP. OF DIJON MUSTARD

DIRECTIONS:

1. BOIL YOUR POTATOES UNTIL THEY ARE TENDER. DRAIN THEM, AND COOL. CHOP ONCE COOLED. PLACE IN LARGE BOWL.

2. ADD IN THE ONIONS, BACON, TOMATOES, AND BASIL.

3. MIX IT THOROUGHLY.

4. MIX IN THE REST OF THE INGREDIENTS.

5. ADD THE POTATO MIX AND TOSS IT.

6. REFRIGERATE IT FOR HOURS UNTIL IT IS CHILLED.

NUTRITIONAL INFORMATION PER SERVING

CALORIES: 217   FAT: 5G   CARB 30G   PRO 5G

Greek Salad

INGREDIENTS:

1 CUCUMBER – DICED

2 LARGE TOMATOES – DICED

½ CUP OF RED ONION – SLICED THIN

½ CUP OF GREEN BELL PEPPER – SLICED THIN

1 CUP OF FETA CHEESE

2 TBSP. OF OREGANO

2 TSP. OF LEMON JUICE

2 TBSP. OF OLIVE OIL

DIRECTIONS:

1. IN A MEDIUM-MIXING BOWL, LAYER IT WITH CUCUMBERS, ONION, TOMATOES, PEPPER, AND THE FETA CHEESE.
2. SPRINKLE IT WITH OREGANO.
3. DRIZZLE IT WITH LEMON JUICE AND THE OLIVE OIL.
4. SEASON IT WITH SALT AND PEPPER.

NUTRITIONAL INFORMATION PER SERVING

CALORIES: 124 FAT: 7G   CARB 6G   PRO 10G

Walnut Chicken Salad

INGREDIENTS:

1 ½ POUNDS OF CHICKEN BREAST – CUBED

½ CUP OF MAYONNAISE – REDUCED FAT

1/3 CUP OF YOGURT – PLAIN, FAT FREE

1 TBSP. OF LIME JUICE

½ TSP. OF GINGER – GROUND

½ TSP. OF SALT

¼ TSP. OF PEPPER

½ CUP OF RED ONION – CHOPPED

1 MANGO – PEELED

¾ CUP OF SEEDLESS GRAPES – HALVED

½ CUP OF WALNUTS – CHOPPED

DIRECTIONS:

1. BOIL CHICKEN UNTIL COOKED. COOL AND CHOP YOUR CHICKEN INTO PIECES.

2. WHISK THE YOGURT, MAYONNAISE, LIME JUICE, GINGER, PEPPER, AND SALT IN A LARGE MIXING BOWL.

3. ADD IN THE ONION, CHICKEN, MANGO, GRAPES, AND THE WALNUTS.

4. STIR IT SOFTLY TO COMBINE IT.

NUTRITIONAL INFORMATION PER SERVING

CALORIES: 324   FAT: 8G   CARB: 11G   PRO: 20G

Chickpea and Eggplant Salad

INGREDIENTS:

2 EGGPLANTS – CUT LENGTHWISE, 1 INCH SLICES

½ TSP. OF SALT – DIVIDED

2 TBSP. OF OLIVE OIL

½ TSP. OF PEPPER

32 OUNCES OF CHICKPEAS, DRAINED, RINSED

1 CUP OF CHERRY TOMATOES – SLICED

1 TBSP. OF PARSLEY – CHOPPED

2 TBSP. OF RED WINE VINEGAR

2 TBSP. OF LEMON JUICE

2 CLOVES OF GARLIC – MINCED

½ TSP. OF LEMON ZEST

Directions:

1. Layer a baking sheet with paper towels.
2. Place the eggplant on the top.
3. Cover it with paper towels.
4. Let the eggplant stand for 30 minutes.
5. Brush the sides with olive oil.
6. Season it with pepper.
7. Heat the grill to medium heat.
8. Grill eggplant for 16–20 minutes; only turning once.
9. When the eggplant is cooled off, cut it into ½ inch cubes.
10. Toss the eggplant, the chickpeas, and the parsley in a large mixing bowl.
11. Whisk the oil, vinegar, lemon juice, garlic, and lemon zest together. Pour it over the salad and gently toss it.
12. Allow it to stand for 20 minutes.

Nutritional Information per serving

Calories: 189   Fat: 8g   Carb 23g   Pro 6g

Chicken Lasagna

INGREDIENTS:

1 LARGE EGGPLANT (VERY THINLY SLICED, VERTICALLY)

1LB PULLED CHICKEN

16 OZ TOMATO SAUCE

1 CLOVE GARLIC, MINCED

3 TBSP OLIVE OIL

SEA SALT & WHITE PEPPER

1 ZUCCHINI, CHOPPED

1 RED ONION, FINELY CHOPPED

1 RED BELL PEPPER, CHOPPED

DIRECTIONS:

1. GREASE A CASSEROLE DISH WITH OLIVE OIL. PLACE THE EGGPLANT SLICES TO COVER THE BOTTOM.

2. IN A MEDIUM BOWL, ADD CHICKEN, VEGGIES, TOMATO SAUCE, AND SPICES. MIX UP.

3. SCOOP ENOUGH MIXTURE INTO THE DISH TO CREATE YOUR FIRST LAYER, ABOUT 1 INCH MAYBE.

4. PLACE EGGPLANT SLICES OVER TOP, LAYER THE SAME WAY UNTIL THE DISH IS FULL (TRY TO GET AT LEAST 3 LAYERS. END WITH SLICES OVER THE TOP OF THE DISH AND BRUSH WITH OLIVE OIL.

5. BAKE IN 425°F OVEN FOR 35 MINUTES, OR UNTIL SAUCE IS BUBBLY AND SLICES ON TOP ARE CRISPY ON THE EDGES.

6. LET STAND FOR 10 MINUTES, THEN ENJOY! (IF YOU EAT CHEESE, FEEL FREE TO ADD SOME TO EACH LAYER, OR JUST TO THE TOP.)

NUTRITIONAL INFO PER SERVING

CALORIES: 188 **FAT** 5G **CARB** 9G   **PRO** 22G

Almond Broccoli Chicken Breast

INGREDIENTS

CHICKEN BREASTS (6 OZ., SLICED)

OLIVE OIL (3 TEASPOONS)

RED PEPPER (1, CHOPPED)

GARLIC (2 CLOVES, DICED)

SEA SALT

ALMONDS (4 TEASPOONS)

BROCCOLI FLORETS (4 CUPS)

GREEN PEPPER (1, CHOPPED)

SWEET ONION (1 ½ CUPS, CHOPPED)

CHERRY TOMATOES (2 CUPS, SLICED IN HALVES)

PEPPER

DIRECTIONS

1. PLACE BROCCOLI IN A STEAMER OR POT WITH WATER AND COOK FOR 5 MINUTES; PUT ASIDE UNTIL NECESSARY.

2. HEAT OIL IN A SKILLET AND SAUTÉ PEPPERS, GARLIC, CHICKEN AND ONION. COOK FOR 15 MINUTES OR UNTIL THOROUGHLY COOKED.

3. ADD BROCCOLI AND TOMATOES TO CHICKEN; STIR TO COMBINE AND ADD PEPPER AND SALT TO TASTE.

4. SERVE TOPPED WITH ALMONDS

NUTRITIONAL INFO

CALORIES 356   CARBS 14G   FAT 11G   PRO 28G

Notes

RECIPE

Notes

RECIPE

Notes

Notes

RECIPE

Notes

RECIPE

Notes

RECIPE

Notes

RECIPE

Notes

RECIPE

Notes

RECIPE

Notes

RECIPE

Notes

RECIPE

Notes

RECIPE

Notes

RECIPE

Notes

RECIPE

Notes

RECIPE

Notes

RECIPE

Notes

Join the free Gout & Inflammation Newsletter.
Clickable links are inside of the eBook version
of this book. Or, you can also email
goutinflammationinfo@gmail.com
and request the link to be sent to your email.

If you enjoyed these recipes,
your reviews are always
appreciated! Thank you!

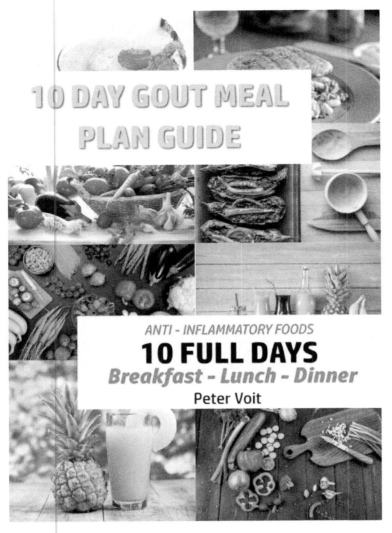

10 DAY GOUT MEAL PLAN GUIDE

ANTI - INFLAMMATORY FOODS
10 FULL DAYS
Breakfast - Lunch - Dinner
Peter Voit

Search for my meal prep guide on Amazon.

I provide a very simple, and easy to reference 10 day guide, that you can implement exactly as is, or modify to fit your current diet plans.

with 10 day meal plan & recipes

GOUT

cookbook

cooking with SPICES for GOUT relief

HR Research Alliance

Looking for some more gout cooking ideas? This book has got some great ideas for cooking with spices.

For some great information on gout, check this book out on Amazon.

This book contains some really valuable information on gout. Look for it on Amazon.

Legal & Disclaimer

The information contained in this book and its contents is not designed to replace or take the place of any form of medical or professional advice; and is not meant to replace the need for independent medical, or other professional advice or services. The content and information in this book has been provided for educational and entertainment purposes only.

Printed in Great Britain
by Amazon

22191360R00057